101 TOP PROPERTY TIPS

REAL-LIFE PRACTICAL TIPS FROM SUCCESSFUL INVESTORS

ROB SMALLBONE & AARON DEVOY

P
POWERHOUSE
PUBLICATIONS

COPYRIGHT

Powerhouse Publications
www.powerhousepublications.com

CONTENTS

DEDICATION

This book is dedicated to everyone who contributed to it. Thank you for taking the time out of your busy schedules to be able to provide your top property tips so that others are able to learn from you. Whilst we could list every contributor here, each contributor (where they have given their permission) is mentioned after their top tip.

This book is also dedicated to you, the reader, for believing in us and the content that you are about to read. It is an honour, pleasure and privilege to be able to collate this really practical set of information for you. We hope that you are able to learn from the mistakes of others so that you do not have to make the same ones.

Your support (and continued support) is really appreciated.

FOREWORD

Getting started in property (or in any new area of business) can be quite daunting. There will be a lot of new information to take in, a lot of people offering a lot of courses, loads of different strategies and, in general, a massive information overload.

Sometimes it is difficult to focus on something when there are so many distractions out there and so many shiny pennies that can be chased.

A wide range of topics are covered and this book really is for anyone who wants to get insider knowledge and advice from other experts in the property industry.

101 Top Property Tips is a complete team effort and leans on the experiences of others, what they have experienced, why they have experienced it and what they have learnt from it.

It is also hoped that these top tips will save you time and help you avoid making mistakes that others before you have already made.

The idea of this book is to give you as much practical information as possible. Some of the tips are very sharp and to the point, whereas some are explained in great detail. This semblance of balance is good and adds variety.

The tips are not set out in any order of importance. This is because they are all important and relevant.

You will note that some of the tips might seem very similar. There are two reasons for this:

1. They are tips that come up time and time again.

2. The underlying story from the contributor is vastly different and thus adds to the importance of the tip.

It is an honour and privilege to be able to share this information with you and we (and all the contributors as well) hope that you are able to take something away from this book so that you are able to accelerate your property investing success.

WHO ARE WE?

Rob Smallbone and Aaron Devoy are co-founders of Devoy & Smallbone Properties and co-host The Property Nomads' Podcast.

Devoy & Smallbone Properties started in 2016 and specialises in buy-to-let investing in the North of England.

Rob is also the author of the #1 Amazon bestseller *Buy-To-Let: How To Get Started*.

The Property Nomads' Podcast started in 2018. The Property Nomads' Podcast is designed to be your one-stop shop for property-, business- and travel-related content. From expert interviews across all fields to handy hints and tips about top books, the Property Nomads' Podcast has it all.

You can subscribe to The Property Nomads' Podcast for FREE on:

iTunes – apple.co/3bHNn5G

Stitcher – bit.ly/3cFQVqe

Spotify – spoti.fi/2XaZliP

Pocketcasts - https://pca.st/63Jl

Rob and Aaron share a love of travel, property, investing and Liverpool FC. (Don't let the latter put you off though). They are passionate about providing excellent content and to help people achieve their successes in both property and life.

TOP TIP #1

Get Yourself Educated

If you know what you are doing, then you give yourself a much better chance of success.

The key with getting yourself educated is finding that balance between learning and taking action.

Too much learning and not enough action leads to analysis paralysis.

Too much taking action and not enough learning is not necessarily a bad thing. You will get a lot done, but not necessarily the right things.

Taking the right action as a result of learning is the sweet spot. This is where you want to be.

You can get yourself educated in many ways. Attend training courses. Listen to Podcasts. Read books (just like you are doing now). Be interactive on social media – find property-related Facebook Groups and get stuck in. Watch what other people are doing and get mentored by someone who has been there and done it.

It is easier, better and quicker to learn from the mistakes of others rather than to go out there and make your own mistakes.

That is how I got started. Investing in a mentor (and various training courses) provided me with a fantastic groundwork. I have never looked back.

Get yourself educated.

Rob Smallbone
www.tpnpodcast.com

TOP TIP #2

Buy Wholesale – Also Known As Discounted Deals or Below Market Value

Ensure you get the skills and knowledge to buy wholesale – otherwise known as discounted deals, below market value (BMV), and understand the numbers and processes involved.

For every 100 houses sold through estate agents, one or two are sold wholesale. For every four you try to buy at auction, statistically you will buy one discounted.

Understand that property investing starts by getting the buying price right, finding the deal, and goes on from there to fund the deal and then farm the deal (making money). Finding the deal wholesale starts you off in property.

We sourced over £45 million value, for £30 million purchase price (before refurb). So:

1. I know that it can be done, and on a regular basis – about 50 a year for us;
2. I know the stats, having done the numbers, so it is a numbers game;
3. I know that from having a discounted deal, you can fan out to benefit in so many different ways.

If you have no money and don't want to take on loans or debt, you can package the deal on to other investors. If you want to earn more, JV with investors and run the deal as a flip. If still yet money is an issue, you can borrow private funds from other investors and buy, refurb, rent out and refinance (BRRR) and pay back your investors. Or, if you have funds, well done, you can do the same – BRRR and pull all your cash back out to build a financial freedom property portfolio.

So, property starts with finding a discounted or wholesale deal, as all possibilities flow from there. Good luck!

Susannah Cole
The Good Property Company

TOP TIP #3

Don't Limit Your Dreams

If you want to do this, then do it. Don't even worry about how you're going to do it – just make the decision to do it. Then, start setting some big goals. And then start putting together a plan and, crucially, make sure you take action.

I meet a lot of people who say they want to do it, but they never do anything. If you don't do anything, nothing will happen. You do need to take action.

And once you start, you're probably not going to go the way that you think you're going to go. But if you start, you will end up somewhere. And that somewhere is probably going to be a better place than you are now. So, my last words would be: get started. Take action.

Peter Jones
www.thepropertyteacher.co.uk

TOP TIP #4

Don't Rush In

"Oh Tej, you have enough little cute single-lets now, when will you do 'bigger stuff'?" – This question irritates me.

BTLs are a solid foundation, but they can also make up the entirety of a portfolio (with diversity). They are low risk, as passive as you can get, and are always in demand. There is nothing wrong with only doing these.

So many people want to rush into development with such confidence (sometimes arrogance) because their mate built one house and made some money, or Dave down the pub said build-to-rent is the best way to become rich. Or, they've been on a course or seen someone's shiny Instagram page who does developments, or they've read the figures of these deals and ignored everything else around it.

Doing 'bigger deals' is great, you can't deny the profit is juicy and maybe it's more fun for some. However, please consider the risks, such as the type of finance you are taking out, planning risk, risk of spending a lot on searches/ground investigations, market forces affecting end values or resales, the duration and delays it can have and more.

Also, consider how you're going to build X many units when you haven't done a simple BTL refurb and discovered the usual issues? Look, it's all totally possible from zero experience, but just consider how you might be better off getting some experience first, and protecting yourself and your investor money by being as prepared as you can be.

Think things through, and remember: 'mo money, mo problems'.

Tej Singh of 'The Tej Talks Podcast'

TOP TIP #5

Do Not Jump Into Bed With The First Person That You Meet

Another piece of advice that doubles up as life advice!

Throughout the property world, you will come across a lot of stories where joint venture partners may have fallen out with one another, for whatever reason, or that the relationship has turned sour and disintegrated.

It is no surprise to hear that these same partnerships were normally formed very abruptly as people tend to just jump into bed with the first person that they come into contact with. If someone has money – great. But do you ask yourself the following questions:

1. Do they have what you want?
2. Do they have what you need?
3. Do you get on well with them?
4. Do you have what they want?
5. Do you have what they need?
6. Do they get on well with you?

Questions 3 and 6 are poignant.

Take time to get to know one another first before deciding to explore business opportunities with each other. Just because someone has money/time/the skillset that you desire, this does not make them a great person to work with.

Property and life should be about creating win-win situations.

Aaron Devoy
www.tpnpodcast.com

TOP TIP #6

Don't Run Before You Can Walk

I see so many investors with big ideas. It is important that investors look at smaller projects, understand the potential obstacles thrown at you on a smaller scale, build the experience, find a good workforce before moving into the bigger projects, development projects, multi-unit properties, HMOs etc.

When you can evidence experienced investing, holding on to properties, flipping properties, you tend to have a lot more options available, more favourable rates and therefore a much better return on the investment.

Liam Johnston
Mortgage Consultant
Kingsway Mortgages Ltd.

TOP TIP #7

Produce A Sound Property Investment Appraisal

Our top property tip is to always produce a sound property investment appraisal that confirms whether the investment will be a success or not.

We have had numerous pre-appraised property deals presented to us, which unfortunately have turned out to not be sound investments once we have carried out our own due diligence in reference to the benefits brought to our client, end user and business.

Therefore, failing to align with our business values to produce quality, healthy plus happy environments for the local community, and guarantee a return on cost for our client.

Rachel Gros
Head of Property Development & Investment
contact@propertyregeneration.co.uk
www.propertyregeneration.co.uk

TOP TIP #8

Don't Get Deal Desperate

You can guarantee that if you become desperate for a deal, one will present itself. The trouble is that if your mindset has shifted from being focused on the figures of a deal to the raw emotion of wanting to secure a deal, then your judgment may become clouded by that misguided determination to secure a deal.

Someone who is desperate for a deal may well reduce their usual levels of due diligence, manipulate their own deal analysis to make a deal fit their investment criteria, and in unfortunate cases be sold an out-and-out lemon!

"You make your money when you buy." – A phrase well used in property, but it is a phrase that should become ingrained within your thoughts as a property investor. Buying properties at the right price will not only ensure your investment is risk averse, but will also give you the greatest opportunity to re-invest further and expand your property portfolio.

Luke Brindley
info@buytoletwizard.co.uk

<u>TOP TIP #9</u>

Don't Believe All The Hype

If you are new to property investing, do not believe all the hype about the fantastic margins that can be achieved from investing in property.

There are many hidden costs that are often ignored by the property gurus offering property training, online coaching and property search for your portfolios.

For example, if contemplating an investment in an apartment block, ensure your due diligence includes a full review of the "hidden costs" in the property lease.

These costs can include:

- Annual ground rent.
- Annual service charges – expect annual increases in line with RPI and unexpected, additional bills for budget overspends.
- Annual maintenance charges – for example, for the lift maintenance, including annual servicing and possible full system replacement (not covered by block insurance).
- Deed of covenant charges – additional legal charges paid to the managing agent for the "freeholder's permission" to rent your property (often overlooked in the property lease), and to confirm that the terms of the lease will be followed.

Why is this our top tip? Because:

- There are many landlords who are not achieving the financial returns they expected because of escalating service costs that were not expected at the time of the investment.

- A number of these costs are beyond your control and there are many difficulties to change the managing agent or freeholder who are in control of these costs.
- The managing agent is not always acting in your best interest, but rather for the freeholder, and they can be compensated with high annual fees despite providing an incompetent service.
- The deed of covenant charge is a scam fee, charged by rogue managing agents and freeholders for an unnecessary document to confirm that the terms of the lease will be followed – in practice, this is not required.

Phil Denman

TOP TIP #10

Emulate Someone Who Has Achieved What You Would Like To Achieve

Emulate someone who has achieved what you would like to achieve, then see what made them successful and implement this into your life.

This is straightforward. If you want to get somewhere, then the thing to do is to find someone who is already there, learn from them and do what they do.

Janice Minihan
Director
Property Transformation Specialists

TOP TIP #11

Set Aside A Percentage Of Your Profits To Build Up A Contingency Fund

Attributable to all business (and personal finance too), always set aside a percentage of your profits to build up a contingency fund and only dip into it when absolutely necessary.

Cash flow is vital to keeping your business alive during tough times. Avoid living too close to the edge. Don't be the naked person when the tide goes out. Always have a contingency fund.

You never know what's around the corner. From major setbacks, such as the 2020 Coronavirus Pandemic, to changes in government property rules and taxation, or tenants not paying their rent, or smaller issues such as big unplanned house maintenance – having spare cash can help you through the situation and out the other side.

That's my two pence! ☺

Jimmy Coppin

TOP TIP #12

Do Not Compare Yourself To Others

You've done it haven't you? Sat there on social media or in your group of friends and compared yourself to others, wondering why you are not like them? Or wondering what you have to do to be like them?

It is a dangerous practice and one that should not be done. It is good to see successful people and to study them, to learn from them and then repeat what they have done. Sitting around continuously comparing yourself to others can have quite a negative psychological impact.

There is a lot of crap posted online about property and from people within the property industry. I am just very sceptical about it and have stopped looking at it as a result. This is because I have sat there for hours and hours and looked at other people and wondered how they got to where they are and how I could do the same.

Sounds depressing – yet the truth is that the time that we spend on social media just browsing and looking at others is time that we are taking away from ourselves and growing ourselves and our businesses.

If I want to study someone, then I will either get mentored by them or listen (or read) their book(s) if they have them.

Don't get caught up in comparing yourself to others. Study them, learn from them and become better than them.

Rob Smallbone
www.tpnpodcast.com

TOP TIP #13

Always Buy The Worst Property Down The Street

If you buy the best property down the street, where is your room for improvement? How do you add value to a value-packed house? How can you make the whole street look more desirable just from your perfect plot? Simple answer: you can't.

Buying the worst property down the street not only gives scope for significant improvements to the house, and therefore a good uplift in value of the house, but the vast majority of the time it makes the street look far nicer and can help the average street price increase too – benefiting not only yourself but also the neighbours!

Alex Stockbridge

TOP TIP #14

Don't Rent To Close Family And Friends!

You should treat your property portfolio as business. As such, do not let sentiment cloud your judgment. Renting to friends and family can seem like a great way of helping them out, potentially forgoing deposits, as they are already trusted individuals to yourself. Or even offering them a reduced rate to show them you're not just doing it for the money.

A tenant who is a familiar friend is more likely to have rental arrears in my experience as a landlord of nearly ten years. There is a saying: give someone an inch and they will take a mile. I have found this to be true.

When you rent a property to friends or family, subconsciously both parties enter into the agreement with a relaxed state of 'client and customer' relationship. You feel empathy towards them, which may result in you going beyond your normal duties. Also, whether they admit it or not, their opinion will now be that you are a cash-rich landlord and therefore can afford more than they can.

Before you enter into an agreement to let a property to friends or family, ask yourself the following questions:

- Would you be comfortable letting them live rent-free?
- Would you be comfortable evicting them?

Anon

TOP TIP #15

Patience In Buying

In the longer term, it's nice to know that you'll most likely have capital growth on your property, as well as the initial capital outlay being repaid, via letting.

However, it is possible to get capital growth in the short term with a wise buy!

Purchasing a property at a low price means you have already got a chunk of equity in the property at the start. This leads me onto the next tip....

Victoria Parkinson
VSP Accountancy Services

TOP TIP #16

Be Ready

Bargain properties do come up – but go very quickly. You need to be able to be able to complete on the property as quickly as possible, or risk losing out!

Victoria Parkinson
VSP Accountancy Services

TOP TIP #17

Understand The Relationship Between Project Budget Certainty And The Relative Position You Are At Within The Project Program

You need to understand the relationship between project budget certainty and the relative position you are at within the project program.

Too many developers think that the initial spreadsheet that they create to see if a project is viable should be the basis for their project costings. They factor 'hope' into the gross development value at the point at which the development is expected to complete. But they do not factor in simple fiscal rules, such as inflation, into the build cost up until the point at which the project is complete.

You need to view a project budget as a range of numbers that gets progressively tighter up until the day the final unit sells. At the outset of a project, if you are having to manipulate the figures to make the project stack ('hope sales' figures and low-ball build costs), and you don't consider a swing of at least 10% in either direction, you are setting yourself up for a big fall.

We consider there are three key stages on uncertainty to expect throughout the life of a project. Through the design period (massive uncertainty), where overall project budgets are subject to cost variations of at least 10% in either direction. Through the tender period (some uncertainty), those budgets are subject to cost variations of at least 5% in either direction. And through the construction period (less uncertainty), the variations can be lower at 2–3% in either direction.

This uncertainly swing-o-meter should not be confused with a contingency pot. A contingency pot covers unforeseen costs on site and during the construction period only; it doesn't relate to the overall project cost. Confusing a diligent approach to overall project uncertainty with best-practice construction cost planning, can mislead investors and result in the need to cut quality throughout a project in order to align with the out-of-date spreadsheet from Day 1.

Neil Scroxton
Managing Director and Architect
Scroxton & Partners Ltd.

TOP TIP #18

Be Patient And Find What Works For You

There's a huge amount of information to take in when you get started in property. People will be telling you "this strategy works best" – but the truth is you need to find out what works for you in your area. What works for someone else might not work for you.

I know people who are really successful at pounding the phone to get deals: they spend all day talking to agents, landlords, investors, etc., and get deals – lots of them. But I suck at it. No matter what I do, I really struggle to get deals that way and it always feels like hard work.

I'm much better at marketing: it plays to my skillset loads more. I can do the work needed to get the marketing material out there, be it adverts, letters, etc., etc., and then just wait for a bite, test tweak, repeat. It's how I built my first property business.

But it is hard to filter out the noise, which is why you also need patience.

It isn't a race. Find your pace and figure out what works for you.

When I got started in property in 2006, I was impatient: I wanted success and I wanted it fast. In the long run, this hurt me. It led to me making bad decisions and, ultimately, led to me choosing the wrong person to go into business with and that led to the eventual failure of my first property business.

Just slow down: don't judge yourself by what everyone else "appears" to be doing; most of it is only half-truths and posturing. It really is a marathon and not a sprint. Slow, steady, consistent progress wins – just make sure you keep moving forward little by little. Soon, you won't realise how far you have gone.

Above all, enjoy it.

Darren Lawes
MyPropertySourcer.co.uk

TOP TIP #19

Build Your Business To Be Hands-Off

Build your business to be hands-off, such that you can continue to invest from abroad. Creating time by not managing your rental properties and using that time to do other things, including looking for new deals, can be fun.

Once we got to a point of a certain amount of passive income, we wanted to start on some of our adventures – e.g. Clipper Round-the-World Yacht Race, conservation volunteering in New Zealand and Namibia. We worked with others to support the business and provide some of the skills, whilst using technology to communicate to do the rest.

We rented out our home as a holiday let whilst "house-sitting". Now, house-sitting gives you someone else's house to look after rent-free in return for you keeping it safe, watering the garden, looking after pets, etc. So, we actually made a profit from doing this over several months.

Being able to communicate and talk through Wi-Fi and timezones really isn't hard in this day and age. As experienced property people, we can even arrange lending, do the due diligence and create new opportunities without being in the UK. We did return to the UK late last year to complete on an office purchase and to get the project underway. Most of the work is done by experts that we either joint venture with or pay to manage.

Bronwen Vearncombe
Property investor, coach and author

TOP TIP #20

Good-Quality Properties Make For Better Investments

Good-quality properties make for good-quality tenants (and less hassle). Most BTL investors are using this strategy to generate a positive monthly cashflow on their investment. The condition of the property will directly influence both the quality of tenants that you will attract and the amount you spend on monthly maintenance.

The properties that BTL investors usually purchase are older properties that will naturally require some maintenance from time to time. A property that has been renovated properly at the start, however, is likely to attract more tenants, as well as require less ongoing maintenance.

The more demand there is for your property, the more likely you are to attract more, and better-quality, tenants. This typically improves your ability to charge a relatively-higher rent too. With a good-quality property, you are also likely to have less tenant turnover.

A good-quality property will most likely need maintenance work less often. This obviously has a directly positive impact on the investor's cash flow. Nothing eats into an investor's profit like constant maintenance expenses.

Alex Demianenko

TOP TIP #21

Know Your Area

You can waste so much time researching a new area. Not all strategies work in every area.

I live in the south-west of England and buy-to-let is more difficult due to high-value properties and lower returns on rentals.

But in saying that, serviced accommodation works well as it is a holiday destination, and in some areas there are no hotels.

Mel Richards
Gold Lake Developments

TOP TIP #22

Research Is Important

Research is important and you want to research the following things for the following reasons:

Property: is it suitable for intended use?
Location: is it in an area of demand? Cheap property in a bad location can become expensive.

Gross development value? Do the figures work? Always base figures on worse-case scenario.

Purchase, Renovation, Profit.

Renovation

We work for many investors that have a totally different working world to our own. For this reason, it is a "must" to use a team you can rely on: a team that views the project as important to their reputation as it is an investment to you the investor. It is necessary to believe your investment is in capable hands and you feel in the loop with the progression and quality of works.

At the same time, your project may have unforeseen problems such as supply of materials, woodworm, leaky roof, damp, etc. In these times, good relationships are needed. A good team will come to you with the problem, but also with solutions/options and costs; if possible, savings could be potentially made elsewhere.

"Man built it and Man can put it right."
"Belt and braces never fail."
– Sayings you want to hear from your team.

Caroline and Geoff Hall

TOP TIP #23

Get The Boiler Going As Soon As You Can In The Refurb

Get the boiler going as soon as you can in the refurb. Don't leave it till last.

We bought a large property to convert to an HMO. It was 200+ miles from where we lived, so we would visit the site every other week and check progress. We have a brilliant builder. He and his team did a great job. They installed a new shower room, toilet room and replaced the bathroom suite. All tiled, all finished nicely.

We stayed in the completed house (another Top Tip) and tried things out.

We couldn't get the mixer shower from the boiler to work. It turned out that the hot and cold feeds had been incorrectly identified and connected. But now the shower room was completely tiled and all the pipework hidden. To rectify it properly would have required the removal of the shower cubicle, wall tiles, floor tiles and flooring!

The fix was to turn the mixer round, so the controls were on the other side to normal and the shower hose connected to the top of the mixer, not the bottom.

It works, but it's not "right". Guests who are used to the correct operation have trouble getting a hot shower.

All this could have been avoided by having the boiler operational before the plumbing was installed.

Geoff Bell

TOP TIP #24

Design Before Development

Our top tip is to make sure you finalise the design of your property before you start any works on the property.

Here's what you need to do:

1. Take a measured survey – get out your tape measure, grab a pen and some paper, measure out every room and draw out a plan – every millimetre counts!

2. Draw the layout of the space as accurately as you can – where do you want the bed to go? Where are the plug sockets going to be? Don't forget radiators.

3. Maximise space in your property by reducing corridors, utilising leftover spaces (like bay windows and under the stairs) or combining spaces (kitchen and lounge) to get the most out of your property.

4. Make your en-suites efficient – you don't want them to be too big and eat into the bedroom space.

5. Use great design to stand out – search for inspiration on sites like Pinterest and be timeless, but not necessarily on trend.

By doing all these things upfront, you can avoid abortive work later on site. It is free to change the design on paper, but the cost of changing something that has been built is infinite.

Many investors / developers rely on their builder to determine the spatial configuration and layout of their project, but how do they know what you want?

Give your builder all of the above information with measurements and you are onto a winner.

Andrew and Mary
Elite Investor Group
www.eliteinvestorgroup.com

TOP TIP #25

Don't Rely On Free Feasibility Work To Appraise Your Sites

Developers, particularly inexperienced developers, need to teach themselves to do the basic work and investigation to evaluate a site rather than relying on freebies from others. You will never receive the best advice possible if you ask someone to 'knock up' a quick scheme for free. It will either be rushed so that they can get on to paid work, or the research won't be done on the site constraints and the relevant planning policy, so the scheme will be too ambitious or too cautious (depending on the risk appetite of the author).

Free feasibilities either leave money on the table or they risk financial loss. If you know in your heart of hearts that you wouldn't do your best work if you were devalued and asked to do it for free, don't ask someone else to.

A better approach is to learn the basics yourself. Understand where and how to get enough information to allow you to understand if a given opportunity is actually viable, and then pay (yes, you read correctly: pay), a modest fee to get the best out of the opportunity and de-risk your position.

You will find that you will be able to discount sites much quicker yourself, allowing you to find the gems instead of waiting on third parties to confirm what you already know (you'll go to the front of the queue if you are the developer that brings partially prequalified projects and pays for their feasibility work).

Most designers would accept only being paid to cover their costs until the project goes live, and you can be confident that you are making offers stack based on sound and well-considered advice.

Neil Scroxton
Managing Director and Architect
Scroxton & Partners Ltd

TOP TIP #26

Property Can Be As Time-Intensive As You Wish

There are many types of property investors and the time invested into their portfolios is not proportional to the size of their own empire.

You can choose to be full-time in property or you can choose to be a hands-free investor by leveraging the services of others. The services of others ultimately come at a cost.

Many people dream of being a property investor, enticed by the undoubted financial opportunities, coupled with a desire to escape their current occupation they have become tired of. The reality is that there are many tasks as a property investor that can quickly require a significant amount of your time. Unless there is a real passion for property, it may transpire that one has simply traded one unfulfilling role for another unexpected full-time job.

However, the good news is that virtually all tasks can be outsourced should you so wish to, providing people with the flexibility to be as hands-on in property as they desire.

Luke Brindley
info@buytoletwizard.co.uk

TOP TIP #27

Always Do Your Own Detailed Due Diligence

It's really important to understand why you are buying the property and who the intended tenant will be. It's therefore important to understand the local area to ensure that the property fits your strategy / tenant type.

When comparing the property to previous sales within the area, it's important to check that your comparables are exactly that – e.g. check the condition of the comparables; the square meterage of the comparables; consideration to the size of the garden / plot, potential to develop within the plot; parking; ground floor or first-floor bathroom; is the loft conversion compliant with building regulations, etc.

If you are intending to make changes to the property or convert it, is it in a conservation area? Is it in an Article 4 area? Has previous planning application been made on the property or a nearby property? These are all factors that can influence the price. Some streets can have significantly-different prices despite being very close to each other. Some examples include: new-build developments next to council estates; a row of bigger houses next to a row of smaller houses; ex-council house next to private housing; a row of houses with great views opposite a row of houses that are overlooked. A flat above or a house next to commercial property. It is only by doing your own detailed due diligence that you will discover this.

I have had surveyors miss issues like Japanese Knotweed and had to live with the consequences, and also mortgage valuers that have reported problems that didn't appear to be an issue on a more-detailed full structural survey

Neil Brown

TOP TIP #28

Do Not Over-Gear Your Portfolio

Do not over-gear your portfolio. What does this mean? Do not have maximum LTV on all your properties in your portfolio. Where you can, go for lower borrowing. Alternatively, start the purchase with maximum borrowing but have a stage-two repayment plan that will take your borrowing down, meaning your portfolio as you build it is not over-leveraged. My thinking is 50% and under. Ultimately, have a few unencumbered properties in the portfolio and some with borrowing for credit-worthiness.

This is my tip based on observation over the years, having started my property journey in 2007. I note the people I have seen go bust in that time have many times been due to being over-leveraged: when one falls, the entire portfolio falls like dominos. Not all cases, but a lesson I have observed and would like to take heed of...

Thanks for reading my tip.

Carlene Clarke
A Fresh Start Accommodation Ltd.

TOP TIP #29

Treat A Property Investment Business As You Would Any Other Business

The mistake that I originally made, and see many others making, is that the sole focus is on the property investment process itself.

"Due Diligence", "Refinance", "Refurbishment", "Goldmine Area" and many other buzzwords in property development circles are all important, but they are very tactical elements of the overall process and miss what should be the key elements of our focus:

- Who will be our customers (tenants)?
- What do they need?
- What problem can we solve for them?
- What is our USP in the market?

Depending on our target customer (tenant), these answers may be very simple, but will provide clarity on the product we are selling and (quite literally!) bringing to the market. My experience is that the more time we spend focusing on this and serving customer needs – as most other businesses do – then the rest will become easier.

As good as it is to find "No Money Down" deals or get "All Cash Out" of the deal, it means we are less focused on our customer and this will be detrimental to our business in the long run.

It also means that if, and when, you seek investment from third parties, you have a much better proposition and something for investors to get excited about in addition to a potentially-profitable property "deal".

I've found that creating a simple business plan mitigates the desire just to focus on the numbers and gets me to think about how I would grow my business in line with whatever objectives I have set out.

Stuart Lordan
Property Investor & Executive Juice Podcast Host

TOP TIP #30

Understand That Being Successful In Property Will Be The Easiest And Hardest Venture You Will Undertake

Before you start, make sure you understand that being successful in property will be the easiest and hardest venture you will undertake. Knowing how to create wealth through property is not hard. Anyone who can add up a few numbers and learn a few basic techniques has the ability to be successful.

But you have to be massively persistent in the application of your knowledge, never give up in your pursuit, deal with numerous problems (including other people having totally unrealistic expectations), and do this whilst maintaining a high level of motivation and focusing on your goal.

Easy, but hard!

Gary Taylor

TOP TIP #31

Know Your WHY!

Knowing why you are doing something is sometimes half the battle. Why are you reading this book? My guess is because you want to invest, or you are already investing, in property and you want to better yourself so that you can add to your portfolio and achieve more.

Having a "why" will be integral to your success in property. It is crucial that you take time to sit down and think about this section as it will change your life and your way of thinking.

Think about some pain points in your life at the moment. Are you working 40 to 50 hours per week in a job that you do not like? Are you working to make other people richer and not yourself?

Are you finding that you do not spend as much time with your spouse or children as you should do? Would you like more time to travel? Do you have a bucket list that you are no way near to achieving?

Do you want to leave a legacy for your family?

Do you just want more money? (i.e. your financial freedom.)

These are some of the most common pain points with people who are looking to invest in property.

Sit down somewhere with no distractions and focus on why you are going to invest in property.

Take time to come up with the top 5 reasons:

1. ....

....

....

2. ....

....

....

3. ....

....

....

4. ....

....

....

5. ....

....

....

If you know your why, know your goals, your visions and what your dreams are. Then, when property does get tough – and there will be days where it does get quite tough – your "why" and mental strength will push you through.

Rob Smallbone
www.tpnpodcast.com

TOP TIP #32

Have Robust Systems And Processes In Place

We all have our own businesses and varying degrees of what we want to achieve and how we go about achieving those things.

If you write down everything that you do in a step-by-step process, then it will be easier to repeat the processes. It will also be easy to hand over these processes to people that you wish to train (if you decide to go down the route of building a team to outsource tasks to).

Good systems are crucial because you will then know what to do at each stage of a process. For example, if you are dealing with buying a property, then have the solicitors been instructed? Have you received the memorandum of sale? Has the valuation taken place?

If you know the steps of a process inside out, then it will make your life easier in the long run.

Electronically document everything that you do, how you do it and when you do it.

Aaron Devoy
www.tpnpodcast.com

TOP TIP #33

Do Not Fear The Difficult Conversations

This doubles up as life advice as well, in all fairness.

Sometimes we get ourselves into very difficult and challenging situations.

In property, this could be having a chat with a joint venture partner about a project that has gone wrong; it could be about sitting in front of a vendor or an estate agent and explaining why an offer is so low.

Too many people shy away from these conversations and fear the outcomes (before they even know what the outcome is). Do not fear the difficult conversations. They will happen. Property is not plain sailing all of the time. Like anything else, there are ups and downs and some days will be better than others.

When having a difficult conversation, I have found it very useful to be short, sharp and straight to the point. Say what you need to and then sit back and listen. You were given two ears and one mouth for a reason. It is best not to turn it into a fully-fledged argument as that can potentially be catastrophic for that relationship. Sit, listen, and come to a joint conclusion and clear plan of how to overcome the obstacles.

Aaron Devoy
www.tpnpodcast.com

TOP TIP #34

Rental Contracts – Getting It Right

The Assured Shorthold Tenancy is the most common form of tenancy agreement for rental properties. It specifies all the details of the landlord and tenant obligations, the sum of rent to be paid and the period of the rental.

There are strict legal rules governing assured shorthold tenancy agreements and your letting agent will advise you on any matters that affect you as the landlord. Most importantly, a professional letting agent will draw up the Assured Shorthold Tenancy agreement and ensure it complies with the law – something that is particularly vital when the tenancy comes to an end and possession of the property is to smoothly revert to the owner.

It is wise to source a sample Assured Short Hold Tenancy agreement from a reputable organisation such as the RLA to compare the terms and clauses supplied within the template your lettings agent provides you with. You may also wish to consider adding additional clauses into your tenancy agreement, to cater for pets, decorating and an annual rental increase.

By including clear and concise instructions in the tenancy agreement, you can prevent issues with pets. If you operate a blanket ban, make sure you include this in the contract. Don't leave any room for doubt. Bear in mind you will have to make an exception for assistance dogs!

Your tenants may wish to put their own stamp on the property by decorating. Whilst this may make the tenant feel at home, it can prove costly to landlords to bring the property back to its neutral state if the tenant moves out. Be explicit and lay out the boundaries clearly, including what the tenant can and can't do.

Landlords often need to increase rent over time to keep up with the level of inflation / cost of living and, of course, property maintenance and so on. Increasing rent can be a difficult issue, especially if landlords have not added this as a clause within the tenancy agreement. Also, a landlord isn't able to increase the rent in the middle of a fixed term unless there is a clause stating this. So, consider a fair and reasonable annual rental increase to include and ensure your tenants are aware of this increase before signing the agreement.

Tadie Hampshire-Haig

TOP TIP #35

Learn To A Point, Commit, Experience And Learn Much More

In a bid to be as comfortable as possible, I think we naturally go through life wanting to know everything there is to know about something before actually committing to doing it. But I believe that this can lead to a paralysis of analysis.

The reality is that we are never going to fully understand everything, so the best thing to do is to learn an amount you feel comfortable with, then commit to taking action, even if you feel uncomfortable. You'll be surprised at the amount you learn through direct experience.

In property, this may be working out refurbishment costs, doing area analysis, writing a finance document, a property investment book, the list goes on...

I would say the best thing to do is allocate a specific amount of time to do research, and once that time is up, regardless of how you feel, you actually do it. This method avoids wasting an unnecessary amount of time chasing an unattainable level of knowledge, and pushes you into action – out of your comfort zone, into your growth zone.

Matthew Fletcher

TOP TIP #36

Get Educated About Yourself As Well As About Property

I've heard it said many times that property is about people as much as bricks and mortar and you are one of these people! Your mindset is key. So know yourself, indulge in self-care and find your way of being the best version of you.

This will give you strong foundations and support you through the inevitable ups and downs that property investment, like any business, will throw at you.

You will have the confidence to reach out to others and learn from them, the strength of character to believe that you can achieve, and the determination to overcome any fears and take action anyway.

Most of all, it will help you to remain in the moment, to have long-term goals but remain present along the way, appreciate the journey, and take the positive from whatever each day brings.

Clare Morgan

TOP TIP #37

Don't Delay Take Action Today...

Education... Property investing is not simply: "I'm going to invest into buy-to-let property, but to do this I need money." NO!!!! You're WRONG!!!! This is the old way of thinking.

I got caught up in the old way to do mind-set myself and it cost me hundreds of thousands of pounds, but mostly eight years of wasted time. Grow a business, make it successful, sell the business and use the funds to invest into BTL properties – that's the professional advice I was given and that's what I did. Until the day my business failed.

Whereas, before I even started to grow my business, I had accidentally completed a Lease Purchase Option on a property I was renting. If only I had known then what I had stumbled into, who knows what my property portfolio would be like today... So START TODAY!

Layton Barr

TOP TIP #38

Learn How To Recover Money From People

In property, there will be a lot of people who think it is OK not to pay a landlord for something –whether it is a rental payment or for some work – and these amounts can add up to hundreds or even thousands of pounds.

It would not be tolerated in other areas of work or your private life. Also, it makes people more likely to pay if they know that you will pursue debts.

It could save you a lot of money.

Ian Denston
Strada Homes

TOP TIP #39

Perseverance

Both investing and managing property demand perseverance. It is in my DNA to not give up and I believe that adopting this practice will see others reap rewards.

Since 2004, I have built up a portfolio of investment properties and manage many more. I have faced many challenges in the time that I have invested and managed property: problems with purchases; problems with tenants; maintenance and repair problems to name but a few.

My recent personal purchases have all been purchased at least 20% below market value, and this wouldn't have been achieved if I didn't have the drive and determination, and more so 'perseverance' to achieve this.

Problematic tenants can cause (and have caused) some stressful situations, however I have always persevered to ensure I achieve the desired outcome.

I firmly believe adopting a 'can do' attitude has been my most important trait and I wouldn't have achieved half of what I have without using this. I am firmly confident that most people would have given up in many of the situations I have encountered.

Persevere in whatever your goal is, and you can achieve this.

James Daniel Khan
Rent Residential

TOP TIP #40

Even During The Hardest Times In Business, Stay Calm And Ride It Out

This is the best tip I can offer because there will be times when you face problems, go over budget, have voids, down-valuations and God knows what else! You will want to quit and cut your losses, but the important thing is to stay calm and ride it out.

If you've done your due diligence and tested the market, it will work. It'll just take a bit of time.

Rishi Bhaskara

TOP TIP #41

Don't Be Afraid To Pay For Knowledge You Believe Will Be Key To Your Success

There are so many people that love to pay for knowledge and there are so many people that do not like the idea of paying for knowledge.

Paying for knowledge (with the right person/company) is crucial if you are going to achieve what you want to achieve. There is no harm in investing in your own education in order to better yourself.

Janice Minihan
Director
Property Transformation Specialists

TOP TIP #42

Do Your Due Diligence On Your Joint Venture Partners And Investment Schemes

Do your due diligence on your joint venture partners and investment schemes and take time to nurture them. Property is about relationships. Taking time to nurture relationships is important. Just because an investor or potential joint venture partner says that they have something, you have to question it. Do they?

You might need money for a deal. If someone has money then that is great, but if they turn out to be a dick and the deal goes wrong as a result, then is it really worth it?

Joint venture partners and investment schemes are like any relationship. You have to "date"; you have to take time to get to know one another. Once you have more knowledge, then you will be in a better position to make a more informed decision.

There are roughly 11 touch points that you need to go through before you get to that stage. With potential partners that might be a few social media exchanges, a few phone calls, and a couple of face-to-face meetings (in person or Skype or whatever works) before a decision is made to do business together.

I had a potential investor recently who was very excited to work with me. I said to him that "we will have to date a lot first". That put him off. It is too easy to get too excited and just jump into bed with the first person that you see. Take your time. Study one another. Get to know one another.

Equally as important as the previous points is to set out, and agree, heads of terms on how you move forward together in great detail. Whether it is a Limited Company (Ltd) Joint Venture or just a loan agreement, map out the expectations from both sides, and look at worst- and best-case scenarios. For example, you purchase a buy-to-let with investor money and you get a down valuation on the back end, meaning you can't repay all of the investor's money immediately. Agree a plan for this scenario from the start and agree ways to manage this. Be open about the ups as well as downs of property investment.

Mark Watson

TOP TIP #43

Visit Your Investment Area

Visit your investment area at different times of day and at different times of year.

You cannot substitute an actual on-site visit. Walk around morning, daytime and evening. Go to several cafes. Are there any trendy independent cafes? Chat to people. Go to the local pub. Are they standing outside looking scary or is the pub welcoming and vibrant? Observe who is around. Engage with people you meet.

It is particularly important to visit at night after your day trips. Does it feel safe? Can you imagine living there? Would your target tenant or house purchaser enjoy living there? Put yourself in their shoes.

Can you walk from your investment property to the local shops easily? What if you were carrying shopping? What if you were pushing a pushchair?

What are the schools like? Are there sports facilities nearby?

You need to spend time in the area to get a feel for these things; desktop analysis alone cannot substitute this.

This Top Tip has helped on me on many occasions, but two cases in particular bring a smile to me when I think about them now, but carry an important lesson for all of us.

My first example was when I was completely new to property investing. I was traveling from my home in London to my investment area, Hull, every weekend, to view small, run-down houses to execute the BRRR strategy (buy, refurbish, refinance, rent) as it is now called. I always arrived around 9am and left by around 3–4pm so I could get back home before midnight. Long day indeed. But that timeline never enabled me to see the streets where I was doing viewings outside of the daytime visit.

You see, most streets can look good in the sunshine, particularly when people are out and about.

However, one time I viewed a small terraced house, that was a complete wreck. I was direct to vendor and was very excited to hear he wanted only £40k for it and "was open to offers". Peaking inside, I saw the house was in a bad state. Perfect to fix up. The copper pipes, boiler and fireplace had all been ripped out, presumably stolen. Parts of the roof had been stolen. But as I walked around the street in the daytime, it did not look too bad. I figured it would suit a first-home buyer or a small family.

So, I made my offer, convinced I had found a gem of a deal.

Only a few weeks later, when I asked my builder to visit, did I realise the importance of visiting at different times of day. My builder pointed out that by sundown, that particular street turned into the Wild West, with drug dealers out and about, and everyone else scared to leave their homes. I spoke to a few agents and yes, it was true, that street had sadly fallen into the territory of some crystal meth drug dealers and they were wreaking havoc.

Thankfully, I did not proceed to buy what I assumed was a bargain property. Had I only relied on my daytime visits, I would have been oblivious to this error of judgment.

This lesson applies whether you are just starting out as a property investor or have moved on to become a developer. As I have progressed to looking for small development sites, the same lesson was reinforced, most recently in East London.

We had an offer accepted on a 6-unit scheme in an "up-and-coming" part of Hoxton. Now, if you have ever visited Hoxton, you will know that the area is very mixed. It certainly has a lot potential and there are some really nice developments, hotels and restaurants popping up there.

The scheme we had our eyes on, looked fine during the day. Not perfect, edgy maybe, but it certainly had potential and was walking distance to The City, so ideal for working professionals. However, one of my investors were there for a stroll later in the evening to get a feel for it – and realised that come sundown, it was a pretty dodgy street. I did the same, and realised it wasn't a place I would want to live. And that is now my rule, if I cannot imagine living there myself, I don't invest there.

To summarise, I implore you to always visit your investment area or site multiple times and certainly during the day and evening time. Ideally, during the week and at the weekend as well. You may just see a new perspective on it that could save you a lot of money in the long-run.

Louis Hems
SOTA Properties

TOP TIP #44

Focus On What You Do Have, Rather Than What You Don't

Often, people enter the property market focusing on what they don't have:

"I don't have money."
"I don't have the time."
"I don't have the knowledge."
"I don't have the confidence."

While this exercise can be helpful to address your needs and how you can grow as an investor, putting all your focus on what you don't have can be detrimental to your property business.

Instead, focus on what you DO have:

"I am willing to learn."
"I am hard-working."
"I know someone with savings in the bank."
"I am good at social media."
"I am a friendly person."

This kind of thinking will open your mind to possibilities rather than limitations.

Maryam Rasul
Catalyst Investment Properties Ltd.

TOP TIP #45

Know Yourself And How You Work

Knowing yourself is crucial. If you do not know yourself or how you work or how you are as a person, then that can be quite catastrophic.

I'm autistic and what led to me getting that diagnosis was the fact that a lot of internal and external pressure led to a breakdown in November 2019. Not one of the best experiences that I have ever had in my life but, in hindsight, one of the most rewarding.

That is because it led me to actively re-think my life, my purpose and who I am. That led to an active pursual. Getting the diagnosis was absolutely brilliant. It has put me on a path of wanting to get to know myself as best as I possibly can.

It also helps those around me and helps clients too. It is not an issue for me to say or write that I am autistic as I am very proud of that fact.

Unfortunately, I have lost businesses, business partners and many friends along the way because I did not know this about myself and was not able to communicate effectively.

Do not let that happen to you. Know yourself, know who you are, know how you work and stick to that. Communicate that effectively with others and you will find that things will become a lot easier.

Rob Smallbone
www.tpnpodcast.com

TOP TIP #46

Always Consider Every Possible Scenario And Outcome Prior To Buying

Always consider every possible scenario and outcome prior to buying and this can be documented in a simple sensitivity analysis.

By knowing what the 'worst' and 'best' case scenarios are, this can better prepare you at the very beginning of the project and can provide you with a realistic outcome once the project has completed.

Jonathan Barker
www.truffull.co.uk

TOP TIP #47

You Learn So Much More During The Process Of A Deal Than In The Theory Of Investing

It is a dilemma often debated in property circles: what is more beneficial to a property novice, is it education or experience?

Many will argue you must get educated. Many will argue that education is a waste of money and you simply 'earn or learn' through your own experiences.

It is certainly true that it can be hugely beneficial to get educated prior to taking the plunge into the world of property investing. There are many ways to get educated, vast amounts of free information, many people who would be willing to offer their own advice and also a huge array of property training providers.

Unfortunately, there is no right or wrong answer. It largely depends on the individual and their own self-confidence to go it alone. Property education can be very expensive, but making an investment mistake can be financially damaging.

There is an abundance of information out there that anyone can immerse themselves in. However, being able to put the theory into practice is when you really learn. Once you start going through the individual steps of securing, purchasing, refurbishing, selling or renting a property, it is added to your own experience. These are experiences that you will learn more from than in the theory of investing, as they are personal to you.

Luke Brindley
info@buytoletwizard.co.uk

TOP TIP #48

Build A Brand

We live in the Digital Age now: your personal brand will replace your CV and is the way you will connect with a large number of people efficiently and build your business.

In property, we all want to raise finance or find deals, being recognised as a force of influence. Giving value and taking action will get you both. It takes time, a lot of work and being very consistent, but if you can raise millions from the comfort of your home using just your phone, are you going to complain?!

Pick two social media platforms and document your journey, share your learnings, comment and like on others' content, and get yourself out there. Write blogs, create videos, take pictures, entertain, share lessons learnt and mistakes made. It does not matter if you have 0, 1 or 100 properties, you still have a value to add and people will connect with you more as they see you grow and evolve as a person and business.

Building a brand with integrity and honest will attract investors, give you huge discounts with your power team and suppliers, and make your whole journey smoother. Also, it's great to be recognised at events and skip the small talk, and go straight into the real networking. Get out of your comfort zone, don't make excuses – use social to be social.

Tej Singh of 'The Tej Talks Podcast'

TOP TIP #49

Don't Be Afraid To Ask For Help

Don't be afraid to ask for help. People are generally keen to help others.

There can be this perception that property is a very 'closed off' world where no one wants to help anyone else. That is simply not true. People in property love helping each other out.

All you have to do is ask. Don't be afraid of picking up the phone and ringing someone. Don't be afraid to post things on social media. People do like helping one another.

Janice Minihan
Director
Property Transformation Specialists

TOP TIP #50

Listen To People Who Are Actually Doing What You Want To Do

Don't listen to Aunty Marge or Brian down the pub – listen to people who are actually doing what you want to do.

I spent too long and wasted a lot of time listening to the wrong people – people who didn't have any experience of investing and were only sharing their own worries and concerns. Obviously, they thought they were being helpful!

Once I paid attention to the people who were actually investing, and doing what I wanted to do, everything changed and it all seemed possible.

I was then able to take the right steps towards my goals and the life I wanted to achieve.

Joanne O'Connor

TOP TIP #51

Patience Is Key

It is worth waiting for the right deal, instead of jumping into an average one just for the sake of it.

Many times, I have seen people be impatient just for the sake of getting onto the property ladder and they have purchased a rental property which had an average yield at an average purchase price.

Several weeks later, they were offered a fantastic BMV (below market value) deal, but couldn't move forward with it because they had used their capital to purchase the average property.

Be patient. The right property for you will pop up sooner than you think.

Alex Stockbridge

TOP TIP #52

Go Along To Local Property Network Meetings To Meet Like-Minded, Positive People

Go along to local property network meetings to meet like-minded, positive people and investors with more experience than you.

Surround yourself with people who can inspire and motivate you. Not only will it lift you up and give you confidence, but you will learn and meet people who can help you in your business. I've built up a great team of people who I've met and connected with through these types of meetings.

Generally, people in property are keen to share and to support others. Sometimes, there will be trades in the room too – so if you need a plumber, an insurance broker or mortgage broker, it's a good place to meet them.

There are different types of network meetings. Some are really hard-marketing focused, but others are not. Try lots of different ones until you find the one that resonates most with you. Always follow up with people you've met and exchange business cards. Meet them outside the meeting to really get to know and understand their expertise and to swap experiences too. Often, there's a win-win to be had – now, or in the future.

Bronwen Vearncombe
Property Investor, coach and author

TOP TIP #53

Track Your Cash At All Times

Track your cash at all times. He/she who does not have the account on flow of cash within property or any investments will always end up plugging the gaps rather than building a business.

Most of the investors focus heavily on building a portfolio of properties rather than looking back and building systems to manage that portfolio.

Cash or cashflow – unless you have an eagle eye on either, or both, you will always struggle to make a business out of property.

Within buy-to-let investment, there are simply too many points where landlords lose cash –be it agent fees, monthly repairs, taxation, insurance, mortgage, compliance checks, to name a few, and in some specific cases, single maintenance that can wipe out a full year's worth of cashflow.

Add on top if the revaluation of property does not come back as expected, the ROI that enabled us to look at it as a deal, is no longer the returns we receive.

We realised that the life of a property investor does not end with building a portfolio, but it just about starts once a portfolio is built, to keep it cash-flowing.

Keeping the portfolio cash-flowing each month is not a simple "income minus expenses" equation, but define and implement systems that will enable that equation to remain positive and secure you at least £150, or above, each month.

With an urge to become financially independent, investors underestimate this challenge and many conclude property isn't a viable business in less than two years' time.

To simplify this further, here are four questions to ask every period and ensure you have responses to be able to build your portfolio further incrementally.

- What is my cash liquidity and where is it?
- How easily can I get it?
- What is my cashflow across each property each month?
- What is my debt to equity ratio?

If ever you are unable to answer the above questions with decent confidence, or if the responses do not give you a happy feeling, it's time to take a break from investing more.

Reflect on your responses to the above questions, and then resume investing back again.

Cash and cashflow awareness, and accounting, are the only ways to gain confidence and build your portfolio further.

Sudheer Vatsavaya & Ravi Vadugu
Limitless Monks

TOP TIP #54

Don't Let The Tax Tail Wag The Investment Dog

There can be a tendency at times to tinker with a deal structure too much, trying to squeeze the last few pence out of it through tax efficiencies or, even worse, doing a deal that tight that the only real money in it is through the tax benefits (e.g. Capital Allowances).

Don't let a deal fall over or become too risky through trying to over-complicate matters. Yes, tax is important, and should be planned for, but it should never be the key determinant in how a deal is put together.

James Hadley
Author of "*The Power of Pensions*"

TOP TIP #55

Understand The Seller

People sell properties for lots of reasons, mostly to move onto a next home.

These are probably not the properties you should be looking at buying. They have been lovingly maintained by their current owner, and although there might be slight negotiation in the price, the seller will need to obtain a good price for the next property.

It's evident when viewing pictures whether the property is empty or occupied. A person selling an empty property will be incurring costs and will have an overall "hassle factor" of owning the property. This is when potential deals can be done. You can usually see tell-tale signs of the reason for the sale during the viewing or initially via the pictures.

Victoria Parkinson
VSP Accountancy Services

TOP TIP #56

Don't Fall For Consultants Who Claim They Have A '100% Success Rate'

This is something that we see a lot when selling services in relation to planning approvals. Those that advertise a 100% success rate either turn down the hard projects and only take the easy ones, or they play projects safe to ensure that they have high success stats.

To make the most out of your investment, programme in additional time to resubmit your planning applications. You will leave money on the table if you do not push the boundaries with your first application. You should try for the risky extra unit – see if you can go taller and try to extend further back than others.

A rejection or pushback from the local authority is your sign that you are maximizing your asset's potential. If your project sails through without any opposition, you've probably missed a trick. So, give your design team ample time and don't fear pushback; welcome the fact that your design team is maximizing your investment for you.

Neil Scroxton
Managing Director and Architect
Scroxton & Partners Ltd.

TOP TIP #57

Be Prepared To Push Your Comfort Zone In Terms Of Areas Where You May Need To Buy

Be prepared to push your comfort zone in terms of the areas where you may need to buy in order to make the process work (buy-to-let in this case).

And, if you're based in London or the South East or some other higher-value area, you need to accept the fact that in order to follow the system that I use you may need to buy (in fact, you almost certainly need to buy), out of your own area at a distance.

By the way, that isn't such a bad thing. The advantage to me of owning properties 150 miles away is that I can't meddle, I can't be tempted to manage them, and I don't get involved in the practicalities of doing repairs and decorating, and all the other stuff which investors and landlords often feel obliged to do.

It's true that it might take a little bit more work to get to know the area, but I think people tend to use that as an excuse not to take action. It's not an insurmountable problem and actually I find travelling to my investment area a fun day out rather than a chore.

Peter Jones
www.thepropertyteacher.co.uk

TOP TIP #58

Become The Oracle

One of the best things you can do is to position yourself to be seen as "the property guy" (or "the property girl") in your area.

When you do this right, people start to bring you deals or potential deals and, over time, you have this stream of leads coming to you with very little work.

To be seen as the oracle, you first need to become the expert on your area – know the streets, the houses, the price ranges, the ceiling prices for the various roads.

Then, you need to know everyone in that area – or rather, they need to know you and what you do. Get to know the agents, the investors, the developers, the tradesmen and, above all, the nosey neighbours and the busybodies. They know what's going on: they know if Sheila down the road is having money problems because Fred has run off with Denise from three streets over. They know when old Fred died, his son inherited his house, but his son lives away and it's a hassle for him to come down to look after the place; he's thinking of just selling it to get rid of the headache.

This takes a little time but if you're in it for the long haul, 80% of this you will be doing anyway. You may as well go the extra distance to become the oracle and effectively control the market locally. When people come to you with "problem properties," you can decide what to do with them – buy for yourself, pass to another investor, pass to an agent for a percentage – the options are endless.

Darren Lawe
MyPropertySourcer.co.uk

TOP TIP #59

Do Not Inflate Your Numbers To Make Them Work

Inflating/massaging your numbers is a bad practice. Do not do it. If you do, then you are lulling yourself into a false sense of security and that is very dangerous.

For example, I have seen various property sourcing agents who will inflate the DUV (Done Up Value) of a property in order to make the deal look more attractive to investors. Those investors should definitely do their homework on the deals, but if they take a deal based on just the numbers given and the numbers have been inflated, then the deal will not be as good as it looks. This could easily lead to a bad reputation and that is not good in property.

Make your numbers realistic – be honest with yourself and with others.

When analysing a deal, it is either going to work or not going to work. There is no middle ground. Cold hard analysis is what you need. If you massage the numbers to make the deal work because you want another property or it will make you feel better by buying, I'd quit what you are doing and find something else to do as you'll only get caught out in a short period of time.. The true numbers will not lie and any investor/JV with half a brain will quickly work you out.

Know your numbers and don't inflate them to make something work.

Mark Watson

TOP TIP #60

Think Of The Acorns And The Oaks

Property is NOT a get-rich-quick business. It takes time and persistence. Think of the acorns and the oaks.

You start with an acorn. You have to feed it, water it and nurture it. Eventually, you are going to have a magnificent oak tree. You don't just plant an acorn and a massive oak tree appears the following day.

Property is the same. It is not a get-rich-quick business. You will not start investing overnight and then become a millionaire the following day. Time, persistence and following a successful path of action will enable you to get to where you want to go.

Janice Minihan
Director
Property Transformation Specialists

TOP TIP #61

Allow Yourself Time When Making Important Decisions

Allow yourself time when making important decisions.

“In hindsight” and “adverse consequences” spring to mind. Do not be rushed.

Tim Watts

TOP TIP #62

Research, Research, Research

You can never do enough research.

Better to do extensive due diligence to make sure you have enough information, as you will never have 100% of the information to ensure you make the right decision.

Better to be armed with more information than less.

Ronny Jay

TOP TIP #63

Don't Blame Lack Of Money For Not Being Able To Start In Property

First thing first: I just wanted to say thanks to Rob for letting me write a couple of pages in his book.

I was thinking to myself that next month it is going to be two years since I began investing in property, and I was super-excited from the first day.

I couldn't believe that investing in property is something that average people can do. Lots of people say they don't have the money or time to start in property. My question is: how long do you want to have that problem?

Lack of time and money is not an issue till you look at it as a problem! And I think everyone should ask this question of themselves: *if I want something badly enough, how will I get it?*

When you are the person who is struggling with money all the time, and it has been a long time that you have been struggling with that, it is possible to become addicted to that identity.

To create and shift identity to become a new person, you have to give up your previous identity. You have to became someone new. The only time that the person can shift and change is when that old habit does not serve them any more and they have to change it into a new (and better) habit.

Success is our responsibility. But when you don't have the success, you can easily blame the situation and say, "I am not successful because this happened to me" or "all that happened to me because of my family." You can blame education, government, economy – everything and everyone.

But the moment you make a decision to be successful and understand it's your responsibility, everything changes. You have to expect that there is going to be pain, you are going to be depressed, you're going to be upset.

You have to willing to pay the price – sometimes you have to break something to make a breakthrough to something else. When you want more, you have to become someone who deserves more.

So, before you invest in anything, invest in yourself – because you are the most important asset In your life.

It's all about having a right mindset on whatever you do. For example, if you are joining a gym and pay £40 per month, you won't get a six-pack just because you paid the gym. You have to put in the time and hard work consistently to get the results for whatever you want in your life.

Afsaneh Noori

TOP TIP #64

Do Your Own Due Diligence

Never trust details from others without checking them out yourself.

It's your money you are spending.

Steve Goodhand
www.hullip.co.uk

TOP TIP #65

Always View A Property Before You Buy It

It is scary to hear stories of people who are just buying property without seeing it. Even if you buy 'off-plan' then you normally have at least seen computer drawings and know where the site is and what the proposed scheme is.

There are, and will always be, horror stories in property. That being said, sometimes us investors bring it on ourselves because we fail to do the very simple things such as viewing what we are buying.

Fortunately, I have never bought a property without having at least seen it first.

If you are living abroad and investing in the UK, then you might be asking: how do I overcome this? My answer to that would be to team up with a very reliable property sourcing agent or lettings agent who you have built a relationship with and that you trust. Then, get them to do a live video of the property so that you can see it.

Always view a property before you buy it. No excuses!

Aaron Devoy
www.tpnpodcast.com

TOP TIP #66

Be Careful On Bridge-To-Let Products

Recently, I tried to use a bridge-to-let product to allow me to build my portfolio quicker. There are a lot of positives with bridge-to-let products, but one fundamental flaw.

This fundamental flaw has recently cost me a really good deal: £64k purchase, £8k refurb and £90k end value, in a rental market of £650pcm. With good cash flow, good comparables and local knowledge of the rental marker in the area, this was a no-brainer decision for me.

I was speaking to some lenders about how I could make this happen fast, as I wanted to get this on the market and my money back out to reinvest. It all started really well, with good communications and good bridging terms. However, the lender only uses six solicitors in the UK, which I thought was a bit strange.

I carried on with this as the closest was in Leeds, which is only an hour's drive away. The other little downside is that there is no contact with the solicitors until the valuer has gone round and inspected the property.

This did get the estate agent and seller very anxious as I could not provide solicitor's details etc. They were fortunately happy to proceed, even though it did seem I was messing them all around. I was constantly reassuring them that the lender had got a valuer sorted and had sent them round to view the property.

This is where the main issue showed its face in the deal. The valuer down-valued the property by £10,000 – which is a significant amount for a £650 monthly rental. When I received the valuation, I was sadly on holiday. I was in high spirits so I was more than happy to walk away from the deal, after spending £900 in broker and valuation fees, as this deal was not worth my while.

I then got home and studied the valuation report, which to my disbelief was disgusting. Examples of the comparables used included:

- A valuation on a property 2.6 miles away.
- Valuation of properties with bathrooms and kitchens from the 1970s.
- Properties that were in need of a refurb themselves.

Obviously, being a Yorkshire lad, I wanted to recoup my monies spent on this poor valuation – only to find that I would be fighting a losing battle. They wouldn't even consider looking at the report I had generated, unless I filled out "their" standard template – and even after that they would still not refund any money, just give me another valuation.

As I had said, I am not continuing with the deal. The property went on the market for one day and sold for £10,000 more than I had paid. "Frustrated" is a toned-down way of expressing my feelings!

Moral of the story:

- I believe bridge-to-let products are going to become more readily available in the future as I know another lender has just started.
- Be very careful of them and their valuations because before even starting mine I was warned that they down-value properties.
- Be ready to lose £1,000 if they don't value as per your expectations.
- If you want to challenge a valuation, then seek advice from you broker first.

- Don’t be as hot-headed as me and say you’re not doing the deal; I could have found another lender and done the deal another way.

Jamie Elliott

TOP TIP #67

View As Much Property – Including Distressed Property – In Your Area As Possible

View as much property as you can (including distressed property) in your area as possible. If your area is a city or town, try and view in different postcodes within your price range. When viewing, think who would be your target market. i.e families, professionals , young or older tenants.

You will get valuable experience in viewing properties and learning about what needs to be done. Eg. location of damp and potential causes and solutions. You will get experience in looking at changes to layout and where value can be added. You will get an idea about the area by viewing the street. Some good advice is to check streets later after dark to see what the neighbourhood is like later on.

No viewing is wasted as you are gaining in experience and taking action. Not everything happens at once and if you miss a deal there are plenty out there. Talk to agents about streets and possible tenant profiles, such as families, professionals, etc.

Christopher Evans

TOP TIP #68

Your Journey Is The One That Matters

Whilst you are wasting time daydreaming or comparing yourself to other people, opportunities will pass you by.

Be the best version of you that you can be.

Every person's version of success is different, so focus on your own and you will fly.

Daniel Clarke

TOP TIP #69

Care More About The People Involved Than The Actual Deal Itself

As a deal sourcer, you often hear horror stories from investors who have come across sourcing agents who just want to make a quick pound note. It is such a shame when you hear about this, as it puts off investors from using us.

The same goes for estate agents and landlords as well. It only takes one bad experience to ruin the reputation for that individual. So, we take the stance to care more about everyone involved, really get to know them and what it is that they want.

Do everything you can to tick all of the boxes. Then, in my honest opinion everyone walks away having had a great experience.

Leave the deal at home and build the relationships first.

Clark Gibson
Gibson Jones Property Ltd.

TOP TIP #70

Always Carry Business Cards That Immediately Tell The Recipient About Your Business And Needs

Tell everyone what you are doing and always carry business cards with you that immediately tell the recipient about your business and needs – investors, properties, help.

Conversations are easily lost and forgotten without an anchor to remember your business, what you are looking for and how to be contacted. And don't underestimate the power of passive watching from people who are curious about property who will eventually overcome their curiosity and start asking intelligent questions and take interest.

Ross Chester

TOP TIP #71

There Is More Than One Way To Make Profit From A Deal

When starting out, be an entrepreneur. There is more than one way to make profit from a deal.

Just because something doesn't pay you upfront doesn't mean it isn't profitable.

You can utilise a project for social media and advertisement gains, end profit and leveraging partnerships. Just because you don't get money from it, opportunities lost are a greater cost than the money you couldn't have earnt.

I suggest this because if, like me, you are starting from nothing, with nothing and owing more, then you have to realise that money isn't the end goal. Money is the bonus for helping others. Profits come from forging relationships, helping others and people knowing and trusting you.

The most successful people are known for being them. Not their business.

Be human. Be real.

Matt Colburn

TOP TIP #72

Look To Add Value That Others May Have Not Identified

There is a lot of competition to find BMV properties – as such, this can push up the price. Competition is fierce for refurbishment projects, where value can be potentially added. Quite often, these properties are marketed at a price that reflects the cost of the works required, but once works are undertaken the end value is only the purchase price plus the refurbishment cost, so no profit is realised.

There are numerous ways in which you can add value to a property, that may not be obvious to everyone who views a property:

- Can you undertake a loft conversion to increase the number of bedrooms?
- Can the building be converted from a single dwelling into flats?
- Can the internal layout be improved significantly to add value?
- Can an extension be added to increase its value?
- Is the property on a large plot with development potential?

There is potential to realise significant profits if you can add real value to a property. The key is to understand if the cost and effort to undertake the works will be realised in the end value, and provide the profit margin you require.

Luke Brindley
info@buytoletwizard.co.uk

TOP TIP #73

Invest In A High-Quality Design Team

When you pay peanuts, you get monkeys. Never a truer word was said when it comes to the design of a project.

We are forced to reject 90% of all 'planning gain' planning approvals that are sent to us by clients who would like to build, because the projects simply do not stack. They are either too expensive to build, or completely impractical to build, and it is clear that they were produced 'on the cheap' with little thought to how they might be implemented.

The savings that the vendor achieved by using a low-cost provider are completely overshadowed by the loss in asset value or the loss incurred through waiting for a scheme to sell.

The same can be said when it comes to the costs incurred in construction when low-cost designers under-provide information for the builder. There is a very good reason why good design and good information costs more money than bad design and poor information. Good design takes longer to achieve, and it has a higher ROI.

Neil Scroxton
Managing Director and Architect
Scroxton & Partners Ltd.

TOP TIP #74

The Fortune Is In The Follow-Up

Keep revisiting your offers. Let people know you're always there as a back-up. So many people go through the effort of finding the lead and building the rapport, only to get discouraged by decline of an offer.

Make full use of your lead, set a reminder in your calendar to chase up offers at fixed intervals. Maybe their circumstances have changed?

People like to know they have a back-up and they'd rather sell to someone they have already built a rapport with than a total stranger. The fortune is in the follow-up for a reason. People like familiarity.

Maryam Rasul
Catalyst Investment Properties Ltd.

TOP TIP #75

Split Your Earnings Into Pots

If you are currently working in a full-time job and wondering how to get into property, then I would recommend splitting earnings into pots. Have one for: bills and expenses such as food (70%), social activities (10%), and then put some into a savings account that you cannot touch (10%).

Keep 10% aside for investments. People say that you need a lot of money to invest in property. This is not always the case. What you need is the ability to adapt.

There is more than one way to invest in property that does not require huge deposits. You need money to invest, but you could start with less than £5k. Keep putting money away each month, think creatively and you'll reach your goal.

Lack of money is not an excuse for not starting.

Matt Colburn

TOP TIP #76

Study Macroeconomics And Keep And Eye On The Bank Of England

Loads of people get into property and this is great. What so many are not aware of is macroeconomics and how the housing market and financial system actually works. It is my opinion that it is quite scary once you really get into it.

Whilst it is great to study areas of property, study macroeconomics as well. This will help you to have a better understanding of how the global financial systems work and how you can help to better prepare yourself in the future. This could have an effect on what type of mortgages you take out and how you gear your portfolio for the long run.

Study the Bank of England and the Monetary Policy Committee and check out Mike Maloney's excellent YouTube series on Money vs Currency.

https://www.youtube.com/watch?v=DyV0OfU3-FU

Rob Smallbone
www.tpnpodcast.com

TOP TIP #77

People Before Profits

People will be your biggest problem, and your biggest help, on this journey. You can't build a business or portfolio without them; you can't do every aspect of buying property yourself – as much as us entrepreneurs will try!

Spend time – before worrying about spreadsheets, viewings, and purchasing – to actually network in your local and investment area. This could be physical events, or digitally, or both. Start to build relationships very early on with solicitors, brokers, builders, fellow investors, etc.

This will pay dividends later down the line when you have an established relationship, especially if you invest far from home. The number of people who have helped me out with a wide range of things, and I never had to leave my house, is incredible.

Put relationships first, especially before money, and I promise in the grand scheme you'll make more money anyway. Work deeply on key relationships, get to know the people in your team properly, take them out for a social event (dinner, coffee, etc.) and bond on a personal level.

We enjoy working with people we like; we work harder and quicker for them. You need your team to be in harmony, and to be working their best for you. However, pick your team very carefully, take time, think it through, use recommendations and follow your gut. When there is a dispute that involves money, you'll see people's true character come out – for better or worse.

Don't ever forget how people behaved in those situations and don't be afraid to drop people quickly.

Tej Singh of 'The Tej Talks Podcast'

TOP TIP #78

Due Diligence (DD) All The Way

Lack of due diligence in property can make or break your property investment business and you as an investor.

Property is an industry where every investor has his/her own view on if something works as a deal for them or not. Each such criteria will determine how the investor wants to build their portfolio.

If one tries to copy or follow the other, the hundreds of thousands being invested is being spent at the mercy of how good that other person is.

Due diligence in not restricted to just property, but the expertise of build teams, quality of tenants, calibre of letting/sourcing agents, cash lenders and more.

Here is the critical part. Failure in any of such due diligence directly results in only one thing.

Loss of money – and in thousands.

Unlike other businesses, you can't buy unit quantity of product or, in this case property, at a lower price like tens or hundreds of pounds. That's the nature of the beast.

Buying a property, if you don't have responses to the below questions as part of your due diligence, you most likely will end up building a toxic portfolio that drains out hard-earned cash.

- Is there a demand for the type of property being purchased?
- Is this a property that fits your investment strategy?

- Does the property withstand your deal profile. i.e. cashflow/ROI/money left in is as per what you consider as investment criteria?
- Do you have an exit process should the deal not work as planned?

Refurbing a property, a few questions to put yourself through are:

- Do you have clarity on what work is involved and how much does it cost to the pence?
- Have you qualified the expertise of your build team with references?
- Do you have a schedule of works?
- Are you working as an investor, or are you getting emotional with works or payments?

Your investments are going to be as good as the quality of questions you ask and you qualify them with quality responses as part of your due diligence.

By no means is one going to get this due-diligence process right first time.

Mistakes will be made, but that is where the systems specific to you as an investor and that are suitable to your investments, will be built too with time.

Sudheer Vatsavaya & Ravi Vadugu
Limitless Monks

TOP TIP #79

Avoid Managing Your Own Rental Properties

My top tip is to always make sure you avoid managing your own rental properties. Use 'experts' for tenants find and management; try to avoid high street agents, but use an experienced private individual/team who manages their own portfolio too.

The reason I advise this is that it's so easy to want to save money, but it creates another J.O.B and eats up your time! You also need to have knowledge and experience because otherwise there are risks involved. For example, tenant contracts are crucial, especially if there is a problem with the individual later on – if you've made a mistake or not shown them the right certificates etc., you may then find that you can't evict them. Another reason is that you need to stay on top of regulatory changes, which is very hard as they are frequent.

My aim in property investing has always been to create the freedom that a regular income can provide. This freedom can enable you to do things you've always wanted to do. For example, my husband did the Clipper Round-the-World Yacht race, I volunteered in conservation in Namibia and New Zealand. We trust and rely on our agents to manage our properties and to let us know when issues arise. That peace of mind is critical to us and our business.

Bronwen Vearncombe
Property Investor, coach and author

TOP TIP #80

Become Very Fluent In Operating A Business From All Angles

You must learn to wear many hats at the start, be a good student, learn from people more experienced than you, acknowledge what you are shit at/don't enjoy, and hire people that are better skilled in certain areas than you are, or partner with someone who is the ying to your yang.

At the very beginning, it is prudent to become super comfortable from an operational and numbers standpoint and have a vice-like grip on the business's P&L. Bottom line here is you have to know your income and your operating expenses. Sounds very simple, and it is, but I know far too many in business who don't know their arse from their elbow when it comes to numbers.

Practically speaking, you need a water-tight set of systems at the beginning, and my preferred way to track numbers is using various Excel spreadsheets I have created. There are countless free templates online, but it is worth taking the time to make your own and get very familiar very quickly.

Mark Watson

TOP TIP #81

Regular Checking

There are lots of people out there who will source the properties for you, but that adds to the overall price.

Why not source your own?

Daily checks on selling sites and setting up alerts on these sites will get you to the front of the viewing's queue! That is not to say a sourcing agent shouldn't be considered. There are often a lot of off-market properties they can give you the details of.

Victoria Parkinson
VSP Accountancy Services

TOP TIP #82

Buy The Cheapest Property In The Best Location You Can Afford

People always want to live in a good location – the cheapest property could be one that needs upgrading/renovating or extending.

In this way, you can build in added value to increase your capital value, and always get good rental income.

Louise Player

TOP TIP #83

Don't Wait Around For A Good Time To Start, Just Do It

Do your research and plan your business and don't wait around for a good time to start it – just do it.

There will never be a good time to start or a perfect storm of situations and potential, as if it were the case, everyone would be doing it.

Don't put it off – plan the work and work the plan.

David Johnson

TOP TIP #84

Get Knowledgeable On All The Strategies Around Property Investing, Decide Which One Suits You Best, And Major On It

Get knowledgeable on all the strategies around property investing and decide which one suits you best at that time and major on it. Once you have decided, take action.

Why?

- It helps to waste as little time as possible to grow your business.
- You are more focused and will succeed quicker.
- It is easier to systemise, which then allows you to move to something else if you choose.
- If you get distracted with other strategies before you have mastered one, there is a danger you end up doing none of them very well.
- It helps you to take action quicker.
- Do – learn – perfect – repeat.

Paul Ward

TOP TIP #85

Ideal Purchase: Vanilla Property

The ideal purchase is the "vanilla" property purchase – a three-bed family home with a garden, close to primary and high schools.

We find tenants in properties less than three bedrooms have more of a turn-around in tenants which causes more void and advertising costs to the landlord. We tend to house smaller families with one or two young children, however, when these children grow, tenants in UK culture tend to prefer each child to have their own bedroom.

Our longer-term tenants rent our three-bedroom family homes with gardens in locations close to higher OFSTED-rated schools. The reason behind this is the children's education and friendships can be affected when they are having to move school into different locations, and there is always a risk they will not be able to find the ideal home in their current location when they run out of space.

Tenants prefer to be in good catchment areas for the children to attend nursery through to primary right through to high school and further education. Being able to offer a larger property means if this home is perfect for them, and they are not looking to purchase, then they have no real reason to move. You get what we call "families-for-a-lifetime" – around 10 + years.

"Having a home a family can grow into is far better than having a house a family has outgrown."

Joni Higson

TOP TIP #86

Avoid The "Buy Cheap, Buy Twice" Cycle

When it comes to replacing your kitchen, quality products sourced at reasonable prices are a great investment and this stops the "buy cheap, buy twice" cycle.

As owners of an online kitchen business, we come across competition from all different types of retailers – large ones like Howdens, Wren, and Wickes, as well as local tradespeople and kitchen suppliers.

What we have found is that the quality supplied at large retail outlets isn't great, and the prices given by local, parochial firms is often out of the reach of the mass mid-market.

At KitchenSinc, we bridge that gap by providing best-quality products at prices that are even better than the high street multiples and major retailers can achieve – which, in our eyes, is the perfect scenario when refreshing your property with a new kitchen!

Chris Hazelhurst

TOP TIP #87

People Deal With People So Make Sure To Invest In Your People Skills

You can know every rule and fact about property, but the truth is people deal with people so make sure to invest in your people skills.

People will tell you all about the best strategies, and they may know them, but in property trust is the main thing.

It doesn't matter if they are your JV partner or your builder. If they like and trust you, they will go the extra mile for you.

Jack Shields

TOP TIP #88

Be Clear On Exactly What You Want To Achieve And Do As Much Due Diligence As Possible

Be clear on exactly what you want to achieve and do as much due diligence as possible in all areas.

There are so many strategies available nowadays that many people go into overwhelm, or flip from one thing to another, or jump into a strategy that might not serve them the best.

A lot of deals fall over because people haven't been open and honest, haven't framed up the rules of the game with JV partners, or haven't done enough due diligence into the deal – from financing, to exit strategies, to full costs.

You need to persevere and pay attention to every step of the way with all involved, such as estate agents, mortgage brokers, lawyers and especially vendors.

Andy Gwynn

TOP TIP #89

Stay True To Yourself: There Are A Lot Of Bullshit Artists Out There!

Do not believe everything that you see and read. There is a lot of rubbish out there and a lot of people trying to make out that they have things when they don't.

Be yourself, follow your path and do what you believe is right.

Don't compare yourself to others or get jealous of others. What they are doing might not be right for you and vice versa.

Janice Minihan
Director
Property Transformation Specialists

TOP TIP #90

Find Your No.1 Strategy: Don't Jump From Strategy To Strategy Unnecessarily

We all know any investment property should work with 3 (1+2) different plans to fall back on if things go south. Sure.

However, you need to choose your main plan (core strategy) to become the local `go-to` person. Learn your No.1 strategy inside out and build your investment business power team around it (e.g. HMO, flip, deal packaging). No one can be the best at all strategies at once.

To do that, first find out what you are good at, as well as what and where your passion is in property. It might determine your core strategy straight away.

Istvan Toth
IToth Property Solution Ltd.
www.itoth.co.uk

TOP TIP #91

Don't Just Take Other People's Opinions On Investments, Do The Comparable Reports Yourself

Free sites such as streetchecker.co.uk are available and free of charge to see local sold prices. Call different agents asking them to roughly value properties once you have done them up (also very helpful for off-market sales).

Many people have been 'sold the dream' by property finders looking to make a few quid via finder's fees and buyers have trusted them and ended up overpaying significantly for properties.

Alex Stockbridge

TOP TIP #92

Run Your Own Race And Buy Houses That Work For You

Having a strategy that helps you achieve what you want in life keeps you focused on why you are putting in the hard work.

Too many people, myself included, tried bigger deals because it appeared that was what everyone else was doing.

Build a plan and execute it.

It is your business, so focus on it and not what everyone else is doing.

Ben Green
Praesidio Management Ltd.

TOP TIP #93

For Best Capital Growth, Buy In An Area You Know To Be Good Or Up-and- coming

For best capital growth, buy in an area you know to be good or up-and-coming and, if you can find it, property that needs a little work.

You can use your local knowledge to get the best you can for your money. Good areas always let well and will increase in value even when the market is not so good.

Using knowledge of an area will achieve several things: fewer voids, nice tenants, good rent and, when you want to sell, a great profit – especially if you have upgraded it as well.

Louise Player

TOP TIP #94

To Be As Resilient As Possible

Nothing in life worth having ever comes easy – and what property investment can bring you is superb, but comes with its challenges and its dedication requirements.

You'll face a lot of hardship and negativity in multiple forms – from negative comments from your friends and family for following your passion, to the rejection by estate agents, vendors, investors, councils, etc. And if you let it deter you from pursuing your dreams, you'll never reach success.

You've got to push through, persevere and stay diligent on this journey, because years from now you'll be looking back, grateful that you didn't give up.

Alexander Thomas

TOP TIP #95

When Dealing With Local Authorities Or Utility Companies, Start Early

When dealing with local authorities or utility companies, start early.

My experience with them is that they allow 28 days to respond to your request, then another 28 days to action your request. If they need further info, it's another 28 days.... and so on.

It can be slightly quicker with a phone call instead of email, but you have no record.

Amanda Bulmer-Thresh

TOP TIP #96

Time, Time And Time!

Understand once you've made a choice to go down the property investing journey, go for it.

Time is on your side.

Layton Barr

TOP TIP #97

Don't Ever Force Your Numbers

Always be *realistic*! Don't ever force your numbers to work.

When sourcing a property, ensure proper due diligence is done on the property and that the figures stack up without adjusting the numbers to work in your favour – don't overestimate the rental income amount.

Be sure to account for plenty of contingencies, bad debt and high bills for the absolute worst-case scenario!

The same principle applies to investors buying for themselves.

If you're sourcing, remember: your priority should be ensuring the deal works for the investor, not for you.

Make sure you're only getting quality deals that have strong selling points such as below market value, strong return on investment, high income generating, etc.

You want to source quality properties, so your investors keep coming back to you for more!

Cormac Thompson-Hale
Property Investor and Sourcer
office@thompsonhaleproperties.com
Tel: 07464 968857

TOP TIP #98

If You Don't See Your Offer As 'Cheeky', It Is Most Likely Too High

Buy cheap enough so that if the market was to crash 20% overnight, you wouldn't be left in negative equity. Never be embarrassed to put in a low offer for an investment property. In fact, if you pay the asking price, you're probably overpaying!

Run the numbers on a property and offer an amount that makes the numbers work for you. If it doesn't work for the seller, then move on to the next one.

Eventually, someone will accept an offer that works for both parties, and it will have been worth the wait and the cheeky offers down the line.

Alex Stockbridge

TOP TIP #99

Learn Something New Every Day

Firstly, this applies to every aspect of life, however, it has helped me significantly in property and has advanced the process faster than without applying this principle… 'learn something new each day'.

You don't have to be an expert, you don't have to be the best, nor be the fastest. But if you can go to bed at the end of the day and know you have learnt something new, then that in itself is a success – whether that be learning from reading, educational videos, podcasts, mentors or other forms. So long as it is published by someone who is more successful in that given topic, then you will inevitably drift in that way.

We all know how compound interest works. Amazing right? Well, this is the case for knowledge. Just imagine if you learnt something new each day, for a year, across all aspects of your life: 'health, wealth, love and happiness.'

I'm sure this will drastically impact you more than you could imagine.

Tom Marsh (BSc Hons)

TOP TIP #100

Network!

They say that your network is your net worth. This is, without doubt, correct.

Everyone knows that property is not all smooth sailing, unicorns and rainbows.

So, having a close network of property and business professionals in your arsenal, all whom have different experiences across different sectors, with different approaches, is invaluable.

Tom Marsh (BSc Hons)

TOP TIP #101

Create Value for Others

My final principle is to always create 'value' for others, no matter what task you are undertaking.

I see too many people chasing the shiny penny.

But what I say is, "Why not create value and let the shiny penny come to you?"

Tom Marsh (BSc Hons)

OUR SERVICES

We are here to help you. We are passionate about helping others to get started in property and we are delighted to be able to offer the following to you:

Monthly Mentoring Programme. An online or face-to-face mentoring programme designed to help you to achieve buying your first property.

2-Day Intensive On-Patch Mentorship. (We go through your business, your plans and work with you to kickstart your journey).

Opportunities to Joint Venture with us.

The Property Nomads' Podcast is your one-stop shop for property, business and travel-related content. You can subscribe to The Property Nomads' Podcast for FREE on:

iTunes – apple.co/3bHNn5G

Stitcher – bit.ly/3cFQVqe

Spotify – spoti.fi/2XaZliP

Pocketcasts - https://pca.st/63Jl

Newsletter. You can also get your free Buy-to-Let Deal Analyser off our website by signing up to receive our newsletter at www.tpnpodcast.com

Buy-To-Let: How To Get Started #1 Amazon bestseller by Rob Smallbone is available for purchase on Amazon.

To find out more about mentoring or joint venture opportunities with Rob and Aaron, email rob@tpnpodcast.com

Printed in Great Britain
by Amazon

78024262R00079